T0246995

A Purposeful Heart

LESSONS FROM LIFE'S EBBS AND FLOWS

KATHY C. PATTERSON

Contact information: kcplove6@gmail.com
Published in the United States by Book Baby
Pennsauken, New Jersey

A Purposeful Heart: Lessons Learned is a narrative format compiled from video chats posted on Facebook and Instagram. The content has been edited to conform to accurate grammatical constructions.

The book, based upon the author's perspective and insights, should be used as a path to self-discovery and self-awareness. It is not intended to be a substitute for medical intervention or professional mental health counseling.

All Scripture quotations are taken from the King James Version (KJV) of the Bible.

DEDICATION

To those of you navigating the ebbs and flows of life: listen, learn, reflect, meditate, be courageous in your convictions, control what you can, and give yourself grace.

To my family, including my husband, Greg, Sr., and my adult children, Ahna, Greg, Jr., and Jonathan who, through their unconditional love, continue to encourage and support me to endure to the end.

ACKNOWLEDGEMENTS

I wish to acknowledge:

God, the Source of my life, Jesus Christ, my Savior and Lord, and Holy Spirit, my Comforter and Guide to paths of righteousness.

Virginia Rivera, my Editor-in Chief, whose unrelenting attention to details, is truly a gift from God. Your belief and commitment to this project are phenomenal.

My videographer and son, Jonathan Patterson.

All of those who view, comment, and share my video chats I've posted on social media. Your encouragement and support continue to warm my heart.

PREFACE

Writing is a labor of love, but for me, one that is not easily abandoned. There have been periods of dry spells as well as moments of pure elation, when random thoughts become flashes of ideas, combining to create meaningful messages of purpose, which I believe, are inspired by God. However, my life's purpose is to empower people to maximize their potential irrespective of racial, ethnic, or cultural diversity through love, trust, respect, and sensitivity. The books I write are avenues which afford me the opportunities to express my purpose through various missions.

So, why did I write this book? The answer is quite simply that there was so much more to impart since the publication of my book in 2022, *Thoughts to Ponder: Discovering your Authentic Self.* The process of discovering purpose, mission, self-image, self-worth, and value are life's lessons, allowing for a life of meaning. The insights I have garnered through life were revealed through bouts of love, joy, happiness, pain, betrayal, secrets, loss, and grief. It is my prayer that you will gain personal insights while reading and exploring the interactive journal, either alone, in a small group, or a book club.

Lovingly from my heart to yours!
Kathy C. Patterson

CONTENTS

PART THREE:
EBBS AND FLOWS.. 40

PART ONE

Purpose, Missions, and Intentions

"The steps of a good man are ordered by the Lord: and he delighteth in his way."

Psalms 37:23 (KJV)

PURPOSE MAY BE CORRUPTED BUT NEVER DESTROYED: PART ONE

Let me tell you a story. I met a woman who was really having a tough time. She had six children, some of whom had special needs, a dog, and a live-in partner, all living in a car. I joined a team of people who was raising funds to meet the family's needs, specifically, shelter and food. Eventually, a place was found to provide immediate shelter; however, it was not conducive for children because Illegal drugs and prostitutes flooded the area. The team's initial thought was they could at least be out of the elements if the mother would keep a watchful eye over them.

One day, after visiting them to pay the rent for another week, it became clear that this place was not sufficient for a family with young children. I spoke to my husband about the situation and said, "We have a vacant property which no one is using . (This property had been a safe refuge for a few families during times of adversity.) "I don't want to put these people in this dilapidated place one more day." He agreed, and we offered the property to the family.

The house had three bedrooms, a living room, fireplace, dining room, den, 2.5 baths, a fenced-in large yard for the dog, and a garage. To accommodate them, we agreed to modify the house so it would qualify under Section 8, and they could receive government funding to help with the rent. My husband and I subsidized what the government funding did not cover so the family could have a safe place to live.

Several months later, a tragedy occurred. Their oldest child was found dead. It was reported that he, a fourteen -year-old boy, died by suicide from a self-inflicted gunshot wound. A note was reportedly found in his pocket. His mother contacted me to inform me of the tragedy. I responded by saying, "I can't believe this! I will come when I leave summer camp so we can talk about it." My thought was to pray with the family, provide comfort, and support them in whatever decisions they made.

After arriving at the house, we were surprised to find they were gone. Not only did they vacate the property, but they also put holes in the ceiling to steal the central air conditioning's copper. We also purchased stand- alone air conditioners when the central air conditioner needed to be replaced. They stole them also. In addition, it was discovered that some of their relatives were moved into the garage without our knowledge. The windows were painted black so the inside of the garage could not be viewed from outside. My husband and I never wanted to infringe upon their privacy so periodically checking the property was not something we did. Not good stewardship.

After recounting the story during a bible class session, a friend asked me if I would do it again. I reflected on that question for a few minutes and answered saying, "Yes, I'd do it again."

I don't think allowing someone to change you or your perspective is going to support your authenticity. I'm cognizant of the complications that may ensue when opening yourself up to others by extending love, compassion, and empathy, some of which you may not be prepared to handle. An excerpt from my book, *Thoughts to Ponder; Discovering Your Authentic Self*, reads:

> *"Water, fire, and wind are gifts to us from God; however, it's not up*
> *to the gift giver to protect the gift, it's up to the receiver. If the gift is*
> *misused, the results can be dangerous. For example, if one enters a*
> *large body of water without the benefit of knowing how to swim,*
> *there is a high probability that drowning may be imminent. If a fire*
> *is set in a forest where it is particularly dry, and the wind is high, it*
> *will most likely spread and cause significant damage to the forestry."*
> *page 43*

If someone presents you with a very expensive watch, would you swim with it on your wrist? Probably not unless it's water resistant. It is not the giver's responsibility to protect the watch. It's the responsibility of the receiver to protect it.

There was a time when me and a friend, who attended church together, decided to start a food ministry by serving free hot meals to those in need. No questions were asked or forms to complete. We rented a neighborhood hall for several months with the support of others in the congregation and welcomed anyone who wanted a meal. One day, a man asked if he could get five meals for his children who could not attend. We gladly obliged his request and he left with the plates. Shortly thereafter, we discovered he was selling the plates. This was not the intent of the ministry, so the decision had to be made to feed those in attendance only. Giving meals to go was not prudent because we were obligated to feed anyone who would attend later in the day.

Have you ever been taken advantage of when you offered support to someone, and it was misused? Or did you have boundaries or limitations when you offered the service? There are people who are takers. They take, take, and take. It is important to help and give to those in need. However, boundaries are critical. Several years ago, my family adopted another impoverished family who had mental health issues. Again, my thought was to do whatever we could to lessen their burden.

So, here's the thing: give and serve others. That's the bottom line. The caveat is to not expect anything in return. If I see someone in need and I give them something, I don't expect anything in return. I'm giving from a pure heart, intentions, and motives with no agenda. Kent Keith's book, *The Paradoxical Commandments*, concludes with,

> *"At the end of the day, it's not between you and them. It's between you and God."page 27*

A closing thought: Always give selflessly. You will be blessed!

"... Though he fall, he shall not be utterly cast down: for the Lord upholdeth him with his hand."

Psalms 37:24 (KJV)

PURPOSE MAY BE CORRUPTED BUT NEVER DESTROYED: PART TWO

Question: How is purpose corrupted? This can be answered in three ways. First, purpose may be corrupted by taking your vision out of focus. I've been wearing eyeglasses since the age of four years. I can remember each time I got a new prescription, it took a few minutes for my eyesight to adjust. My depth perception was off. As I walked, I couldn't distinguish where the floor or the ground was in relation to my perception. My vision was out of focus.

Secondly, purpose can be corrupted by diminishing the true intent. What is the intent of the purpose? Is it true to your authentic self or, is it a purpose given to you by someone else? The alternative for authenticity is false representation, presenting oneself differently depending upon circumstances or situations. It is easy to corrupt your purpose by listening to others rather than believing in yourself. For example, I receive many positive comments related to my video chats; however, I have also received negative comments some which were profane. Guess which comments linger into the deep recesses of my mind?

It is critical to believe in who you are and allow your purpose to direct your missions, rather than believe the perceptions of others. If not, falling prey to what others tell you about yourself may result in a corrupted purpose.

Thirdly, purpose can be corrupted by allowing obstacles to distract and determine your path instead of realigning the process. Think about a car's navigational system. The road you're traveling to reach your destination may require a detour but ultimately, you will be led back to the original road. Similarly, you may undertake a project and it may not unfold as expected. However, you must keep moving forward. Don't stop pursuing your vision because there are unexpected delays. Delays don't necessarily mean that your vision won't come to pass. Fulfilling a vision may be extremely challenging. Take the time to learn from the challenge and persevere.

Fourthly, don't let perfectionism distract you from pursuing your mission. Everything builds upon itself. Prior to the COVID shutdown, I wrote a play which had been performed live. It was gaining momentum and the audiences were extremely receptive. However, it became necessary to pivot to online offerings because of the shutdown. I decided to post "video chats" discussing the taglines of the play: life, love, pain, hope, and faith. Vulnerability has become my close kin because of the negative self-talk I sometimes give credence. Occasionally, I ask myself if it is worth the risk to express my thoughts and be subjected to the opinions of others. In addition, I have made mistakes in my postings which highlighted my intention to be perfect. Remember, Voltaire, a famous writer and historian, was once quoted saying, *"Don't let the perfect be the enemy of the good."*

An excerpt from my book, *Thoughts to Ponder: Discovering Your Authentic Self*, reads,

> *"I take a risk every time I post a video or write an essay because I'm making my innermost thoughts known. But, if I am to stay true to my life's purpose and present mission, I must be willing to take a risk, which means I'll be vulnerable to others."* page 34

Moreover, I believe my writings are divinely inspired and therefore not subjected to cancellation. The video chats have now exceeded more than 100 and counting.

So, how can purpose be corrupted? To summarize:

1. Taking your vision out of focus.

2. Diminishing the true intent.

3. Allowing obstacles to distract and determine the path.

4. Making perfectionism be the enemy of the good.

A closing thought: Remember, it's God who gave you purpose, not man. It may be corrupted, but NEVER destroyed!

"O generation of vipers, how can ye, being evil, speak good things? For out of the abundance of the heart the mouth speaketh."

"A good man out of the good treasure of the heart bringeth forth good things: an evil man out of the evil treasure bringeth forth evil things."

Matthew 12:34-35 (KJV)

BE WHO YOU ARE, NO MATTER THE SITUATION.

Frequently, I have met with people who are hurting because they are misunderstood. They are not allowing themselves to be who they are for fear of making someone else feel uncomfortable or not being accepted into a particular group. Why? It is because their self-perception has been formed and rooted in the opinions of others. Does it serve anyone well to be fake and self-sabotage his or her own sense of true identity?

I coined a term called, *SWID, Self-Worth Image Disorder*. It is caused by such attributes as physical, sexual, emotional, and/or mental abuse, abandonment, rejection, addictions, to name a few. *SWID* may become solidified in one's psyche by negative self-talk which can lead to self-doubt. Thoughts like,"Who do you think you are? Who told you your opinions are valuable? Who cares what you think? Why do you insist upon injecting your thoughts into the lives of others?" It is imperative to silence negative self-talk because it can damage self-esteem.

Unfortunately, many people, including myself, have been afflicted by the "people-pleasing" disease. The problem is another person's opinion about who you are may not be based upon pure motives. Their agenda may be character assassination. It is dangerous to rely upon the opinions of others to tell you your self-worth or self-perception. A person's opinion of you may change if there is a breach in the relationship or if you are no longer valued. Consequently, self-discovery affirms authenticity and negates imitation. The journey may not be easy, but necessary. It's daunting to admit that there may be situations in your past that reflect poorly on your character. Life is a school and lessons occur each day. Things change which can result in painful experiences. However, the way these situations are handled will determine the consequences of your actions.

Interestingly, there are those who say, "*This is me; like it or not!*". According to Wikipedia, many years ago, a popular comic strip based upon the fictional character, *Popeye the Sailor*, created by Elzie Crisler Segar, was famously quoted as saying, 'I yam what I yam an' tha's all I yam." Adapting Popeye's mantra is great when your authenticity is founded in the person God created you to be.

> "*But the fruit of the Spirit is love, joy, peace, longsuffering, gentleness, goodness, faith,*
> *Meekness, temperance: against such there is no law.*"
> *Galatians 5:22-23 (KJV)*

In addition, compassion, empathy, and sympathy for humanity become integral to your personality. However, I've met those who declare their actions are emblematic of their authenticity which does not represent the above-mentioned traits. If they say, "*This is just who I am, take it or leave it*", accept it and be forewarned that they may cause devastation, confusion, and hostility in their presence.

Maya Angelou, a wise woman, poet laureate, and so much more, once said, "*When a person shows you who they are, believe them because they know themselves better than you.*" Their expressions are of the heart, their very essence. They may be mean, chaotic, toxic, volatile, the antithesis of the virtues listed in Galatians, as well as agents of character assassination, having others dislike and castigate another based upon the former's disdain, not nice to be around. Authenticity can only be inferred by one's actions.

A closing thought: Always be who you are by presenting to the world an authentic person created by God. Your essence should exemplify your personality, character, and goodwill to all men. Declare that you will not shrink to feed the esteem of others or negotiate your essence to fit in. There is a caveat to this discussion; To be authentic, take a journey into self-awareness, self-discovery, and introspection. Seek God in all you do and always ask for His guidance.

"And you shall know the truth, and the truth shall make you free. ...If the Son therefore shall make you free, ye shall be free indeed."

John 8:32;36 (KJV)

I KNOW WHO I AM –
NO NEGOTIATION EVER!

There are a few authors I enjoy reading, Dr. Brene Brown being among them. Her research focuses on vulnerability and shame. As I was perusing some of her interviews, she said,

> *"Our worth and our belonging are not negotiated with other people...I will negotiate a contract with you, I will negotiate maybe even a topic with you, but I'm not going to negotiate who I am with you...because... then I may fit in for you but I no longer belong to myself and that is a betrayal I am not willing to do anymore."*

This resonated with me because I have allowed myself to become a "people pleaser" during times in my life. It mattered to me what other people thought about me, whether they knew me or not.

Several years ago, I became acquainted with a long - distance family member. We formed a relationship and got to know each other. During one of our conversations, she said, "You know what, I didn't like you." I responded in bewilderment, "Really, why not?" Her reason was not because she knew me or the result of something I did to her. It was due to the character assassinations perpetrated against me by other family members. Essentially, her dislike for me was formed through the eyes of others. It is critical for self-discovery to take precedence in our psyche so it can facilitate the continual knowledge and constant growth of self-perception. It connects one's self-awareness to self-worth, self-reflection, introspection, and rejuvenation.

How many times do you enter a situation where you are cognizant of those who may not have your best interests at heart? Do you shrivel up, disappear into the atmosphere, and diminish your God-given traits? Is it worth it to suppress your uniqueness to assimilate into what others have forced upon you or be your yourself? Unfortunately, there are those whose desire to be accepted by others outweighs the authenticity of themselves. The inclination is to show up as an imitation and hide the brilliance God has placed within, ultimately becoming unrecognizable even to themselves.

I'm reminded of the difference between camouflage and metamorphosis. The octopus, an extremely intelligent animal, can camouflage itself so that it takes on the very nature of the environment, meaning it can reverse the condition and return to its original state when the danger is gone. On the other hand, the caterpillar becomes a butterfly through the process of metamorphosis meaning a total transformation takes place. It is forever changed. I find it necessary to say this again: you are valuable, you are worthy, you are amazing, you are incredible, and you are loved!

Never allow your self-perception to be formed by the opinions of others. God's opinion is the only one that matters. Seek Him to find the truth of whom He created you to be. Honestly, be careful of your own opinion because it can be relegated to past mistakes or self-doubt.

It has become clear that several events contributed to a self-diagnosis of SWID. Beginning in the 1960's, sexual molestation; 1970's, my paternity was revealed; 1980's, breaches in family, church, and friendship relationships; 1990's, my mother became ill, never recovered, causing a period of isolation; 2,000's, business, and financial losses because of Hurricane Katrina. Consequently, many years ensued before I could move forward, remembering God's promises to never leave me nor forsake me.

Malcolm Gladwell wrote in his book, *The Outliers,*

"The tallest oak in the forest is the tallest not just because it grew from the hardiest acorn. It is the tallest also because no other trees blocked its sunlight, the soil around it was deep and rich, no rabbit chewed through its bark as a sapling and no lumberjack cut it down before it matured." page 19

I believe that some were raised in heinous situations which negatively impacted areas of their lives while others came from stable homes which propelled them into great paths. However, know that circumstances may not determine outcomes.

A sister-friend once told me she came to the earth to learn "faith". My word is love, which is why I've been in many unloving situations. I am attuned to people who are behaving unlovingly as well as those who are loving. I am grateful that God's love has sustained me through the years.

A closing thought: Respecting another person's perception of your worth and value is dangerous since it may change. Understand who you are and refuse to negotiate it with anyone. Stand firm and focus on your purpose and the missions God has assigned to your hands. Be resolute and determined to follow your path and don't change for anyone.

"A ship in a harbor is safe, but that is not what a ship is built for."

William Shed

REFLECT AND MEDITATE

Vulnerability is real and can uproot one's confidence. During the writing process, my self-talk has ranged from, "I'm in my creative zone and there isn't anything that can stop me" to "Who cares what you think", or "Why should someone listen to you?" I have felt like I can scale the highest summit on Mount Everest to the doldrums of one sinking in quicksand. However, when purpose is cemented in your spirit and the mission is given, the only choice is to stand erect, square your shoulders, take a deep breath, and stay focused on your pursuit.

Once recognizing the power of vulnerability, I have also given into fear. The fear of rejection may be the strongest deterrent as the basis of unrealized potential. One of the questions I have posed before is, "Are you willing to take a risk to be vulnerable? If your answer is "Yes", then what or who is stopping you? Fear is one of the most destructive enemies that may prevent you from following your purpose, vision, mission, dreams, and goals.

Let's reflect on this thought. If a seed is planted, it may be forgotten once in the soil. One day, a sprout appears. Why? Because it has been nurtured by being provided sunlight or, depending upon its needs, put in a cool environment, given water, and plant food. Obviously, there were processes happening beneath the soil although you didn't see them.

Using the above discussion to form an analogy, what are you doing regarding pursuing a mission? What processes are you following? Are you keeping your head down and pushing forward irrespective of the challenges on your path? Will you allow fear to thwart it? What about people who tell you there is no merit to your endeavors (I call these people "dimmers")?

Always remember that it is your purpose that determines your mission which should align with your purpose. This sets up your priorities which necessitate organization. In addition, purpose helps you to remain confident while persevering in your God-given assignments.

A closing thought: You are a gift to the world, one to be treasured. Pursue your missions with reckless abandonment and never retreat. The world is waiting to be introduced to you!

"Let all bitterness, and wrath, and anger, and clamour, and evil speaking, be put away from you, with all malice:
And be ye kind one to another, tenderhearted, forgiving one another, even as God for Christ's sake hath forgiven you."

Ephesians 4:31-32 (KJV)

BETRAYAL OF LOVE: STAY TRUE TO YOURSELF

What happens when love is unrequited, a love that is not returned? What happens to self-image when love is unrequited? Many have given love to others and had it trampled over, leaving a heap of ashes in their hearts. Can the remnants be removed, and the area swept clean or are the memories embedded forever leaving a trail of pain? It may be damaging to the emotional well-being of the person who loved freely. It can be painful, signaling negative self-talk which underscores negative self-image.

My greatest disappointments in life have been when I extended agape love to others, be it family or friend relationships, and it wasn't received or returned. Life has thrown me into many unloving situations which were heartrending at best. I've postulated the thought that perhaps the opposite of love is suffering rather than hate. Hate may be a manifestation of the suffering one feels. The challenge is to remain who you are and not let others turn you into someone with a hardened heart.

I am resolved to be a loving being committed to spreading love to others. I will not be a conduit of chaos, confusion, hypocrisy, or deceit. God has created me to be a loving being designed to serve others. I will not partake in a toxic or hostile environment wherever I find myself. There are those who may attempt to sabotage your relationships with other because of their disdain for you, sometimes because of their lack of self-love. Be careful that how you feel about yourself is not tainted by what others have said or perpetrated against you and your character. Spread love and kindness whether it is unrequited or not!

A closing thought: On October 4, 1993, while attending a Vision Conference in New Orleans, La., I became free from the opinions of others. As the late Dr. Myles Munroe preached. Since that day, I have endeavored to love others whether it is unrequited or not. I say to you - just love. Do it anyway!

PART TWO

Reflect and Meditate

"He who passively accepts evil is as much involved in it as he who helps perpetuate it."

Dr. Martin Luther King, Jr.

THE STRENGTH OF COURAGE IS DETERMINED BY THE DEPTHS OF ONE'S CONVICTIONS

Recently, I read the story of *"The pig and the sheep"*, a fable in Jerry Pinkney's book, *Aesop Fables*. To summarize, a shepherd, who was tending to his sheep, found a pig huddled amongst them. He decided to sell the pig for a great amount of money. As he was carrying the pig under his arm, the pig began thrashing, kicking, and screaming. One of the sheep was annoyed by the pig's actions and asked,

> *"What a fuss you're making!" scolded one elderly sheep. The shepherd often carries one of us away, but you'd never see a sheep whimper like that. Show a little courage. Easy for you to say gasped the frightened pig! When the shepherd carries you away, he only wants your wool. But when he wants bacon, that will be the end of me."*
> *"The moral of the fable is it's easy to speak of courage when you're safe and sound." page 36*

The sheep was comfortable and didn't need courage. Giving up his wool didn't require giving up his life. The pig, on the other hand, would have to give up his life to provide bacon for breakfast.

During the height of the January 6th assault on the United States Capitol in 2021, Eugene Goodman, a capitol policeman, acted with undeniable courage when he helped Congress get to safety. He wasn't safe. No one was safe. It was reported that the crowd even chanted, *"Hang Mike Pence!"*, former Vice President of the United States, during the attack. However, Mr.

Goodman stood on his principles and was faithful to the oath he pledged when he was sworn in as a member of law enforcement.

Frequently, standing on your convictions may require courage and bravery in the face of overwhelming pressure to fall in line with the majority opinions. You may be in the minority or alone when someone speaks undesirably about another and you refuse to participate in the lambasting. It takes courage to be firm in your convictions when your opinions are challenged.

I'm reminded of one of the late former President of the United States of America, John F. Kennedy's, favorite quotes by Dante, an Italian poet, political thinker, and moral philosopher, which he referenced in his book, *Profiles in Courage.*

"The hottest places in Hell are reserved for those who, in times of great moral crisis, maintain their neutrality", wrote Dante. *page xvii*

Deciding to remain steadfast in your convictions may not be easily attained, but it will make it much more palatable to tolerate your reflection in a mirror.

A closing thought: Look in the mirror, gaze upon your reflection declaring to one and all, "I know who I am. I will not fall for other people's opinions about me. I will stand firm on my convictions, never vacillating.

"There may be four things which are little upon the earth, but they are exceeding wise:
The ants are a people not strong, yet they prepare their meat in the summer;
The conies are but a feeble folk, yet they make their houses in the rocks;
The locusts have no king, yet go they forth all of them by bands;
The spider taketh hold with her hands, and is in kings' palaces."

Proverbs 30:24-28(KJV)

PURPOSE, MISSION, AND INTENTIONS

One evening, as I was walking in my neighborhood, I was reflecting on self-discovery. My spirit was alive with the thoughts that I am a loving being determined to be a vessel of love and peace declaring I will not bring harm to others. I am not a vessel of hate, chaos, confusion, or malice toward others.

My thoughts ultimately focused on my life's purpose which is to empower people to maximize their potential irrespective of racial, ethnic, or cultural diversity through love, trust, respect, and sensitivity. What became clearer was that purpose is different from mission. For example, my missions are to spread love, self-awareness, introspection, and self-discovery. Do these entities align with my purpose? Absolutely, because they are empowering. To reiterate, missions should always align with purpose.

Years ago, I was a member of a congregation where some in leadership became disgruntled with me based upon the opinions of those who began a campaign of character assassination. After being involved in many of the church's activities, where I was lauded by some and castigated by others, I was silenced, and looked upon as a renegade. Prior to this time, I had spoken on many programs, taught classes during conferences, and was an adult counselor of the youth department. Incidentally, I had also authored two books.

There was a Black History program where a participant was asked to spotlight an African American author. She prefaced her remarks by stating that she had been contemplating on what author to feature when her choice was made. She proclaimed, "As I was coming down my stairs, it suddenly occurred to me that we had one right here." To my amazement, she began to read from my book, I am a Jewel. It was stunning to hear my words read aloud when I had been silenced. God uses whom He chooses to bless you by using another in your stead when you are not received.

"...Thou preparest a table before me in the presence of mine enemies; thou anointest my head with oil; my cup runneth over." Psalms 23:5)KJV)

I heard God whispering in my ear, "I am here even when you think I'm not."

A closing thought: Discover your purpose and remain true to it. You may feel inadequate or question your ability to complete your missions. There may be those who will give you a negative prophecy saying you don't have the capability or aptitude to be successful in your endeavor. Forge ahead anyway. God has equipped you with all that you need.

"Let brotherly love continue.

Be not forgetful to entertain strangers: for thereby some have entertained angels unaware."

Hebrews 13: 1-2 (KJV)

BE MINDFUL OF YOUR DAILY WALK

Mahatma Gandhi, a Hindu who practiced Buddhism, was instrumental in a nonviolent movement for human rights in his country of India. He was quoted as saying, "*I would have become a Christian had it not been for the Christians.*" It was certainly a negative stain on Christianity. Being intrigued by his comment, I researched to find out why he made such a remark.

My research led me to an article in the *Kansas City Star*, a digital periodical, which was updated in January 2021. It was reported that Gandhi had become enthralled with those who worshipped Jesus and desired to learn more about the faith. He decided to visit a Christian church in Calcutta, India whereupon he was denied entrance. Recognizing that India divided its citizenry by race and social class, it was explained that this church was only for "high caste elites and white soulmates." The article ended with, "*Gandhi rejected the Christian faith never again to consider the claims of Christ.*"

As you take the journey into introspection, reflect on whether your "faith walk" mirrors your "faith talk", your profession of faith. Humans are flawed beings because of birth. *Psalms 51:5 (KJV)* says,

"*Behold I was shapen in iniquity; and in sin did my mother conceive me.*"

Unfortunately, some of life's decisions are made which are antithetical to the precepts of Christianity in which a Christian should abide. Are you known by your values and the integrity of your character?

Several years ago, my husband and I adopted a poor family consisting of a father, mother, and two children. I recounted my experience with the mother in my book, *I am a Jewel.*

> *"During several conversations with the mother which followed in the days to come, I discovered that she had birthed six children, four of whom were taken by the state because of neglect. She was living in a condemned building with her common-law husband who attempted to support the family by recycling cans and cleaning construction sites. Later, she told me she had been raped more than once, beaten, and left on a city street and violated in every conceivable way. Her mental health was indeed compromised." page 22*

We would take the family to the church we attended at the time, where they were frequently looked upon with disgust. It was no secret how some of the congregants felt about their presence in the church. One Sunday after service, a woman handed me a bag of clothes to give to the mother, saying she would never wear them herself, but the mother would appreciate them. Her facial expression appeared to reveal a look of "I'm better than that woman." It was apparent that she believed the mother to be "less than". Did she know the adversities the mother had faced? No, but I don't believe it would have mattered. I took the clothes, thanked her, and immediately put them in the garbage can.

So, what does it look like to have a lifestyle of evangelism? What does a "faith walk" look like? Would someone say after meeting you, "I'd like to know more about Christianity and Jesus Christ?" What do you look like to those around you? A friend said something profound to me when she declared "I don't have to title myself, other people will title me." What title will others bestow upon you?

A dear friend shared a Facebook post with me which referenced a pastor who was about to become head pastor of a congregation. Prior to introducing himself, he dressed like a homeless man and went to the church. Guess what happened? The congregation ignored him. He asked for money, but no one acquiesced. This story resonated with me deeply because I wrote a play based upon a dream about Jesus attending a church celebration. After arriving, he was immediately escorted by men who were dressed in black suits and white shirts. They restricted his movement with shackles and by holding his arms tightly in a way that was reminiscent of what police guards would do when escorting prisoners. The play was interactive, so the characters were seated among the congregation without their knowledge.

During the play, each character would stand and give their testimonies, ending with, "I know Him! Do you really know Him?" The refrain was the same for the prostitute, gang member, sexual abuse survivor, domestic abuse survivor, and one diagnosed with depression. The finale ended with Jesus dropping the shackles and showing himself to the congregation. The play reminded us that there are those who profess Christ but don't really know Him.

There was another memorable incident that happened one Sunday as my family was arriving for the service. A man, who appeared to be homeless, was in front of the church asking those arriving to give him money, but everyone ignored him. I was bothered by this interaction, so I gave him money and went into church. During the service, I was astonished to see the same man come up the center aisle and put the money I gave him in the offering plate. My heart was truly warmed.

A closing thought: Our profession of faith must always be made manifest. Love for humanity is essential to an authentic faith-walk. What is your lifestyle? Is it emblematic of your Christian faith? Each day, God gives us an opportunity to transform into a follower of Christ, one who is compassionate, kind, a doer of all that is good, extending love and encouragement to others. Just asking…

"So shalt thou find favour and good understanding in the sight of God and man.

Trust in the Lord with all thine heart; and lean not unto thine understanding.

In all thy ways acknowledge him, and he shall direct thy paths."

Proverbs 3:4-6 (KJV)

THE POWER OF ONE

I have been invited to be a presenter at several educational conferences during my career as a Speech-language Pathologist. I would typically begin the session with a quote by Haim Ginott, author of *Teacher and Child*, which says,

> *"I've come to the frightening conclusion that I am the decisive element in the classroom.*
>
> *It's my personal approach that creates the climate. It's my daily mood that makes the weather as a teacher. I possess a tremendous power to make a child's life miserable or joyous. I can be a tool of torture or an instrument of inspiration. I can humiliate or heal in all situations. It is my response that decides whether a crisis will be escalated or de-escalated, and a child humanized or dehumanized." page 15*

Thus, the power of one.

Another instance of the power of one was illustrated on a *CBS Sunday Morning* episode. Doreen Ketchens, a jazz clarinetist, who plays music on a corner in the French Quarter in New Orleans, Louisiana, was recorded by someone and posted the video on social media. During her interview on CBS Sunday Morning, the journalist asked Doreen what would she like to do in the future. She responded that she would like to play at a New York venue. As fate would have it, a man with connections in New York, contacted a venue and Doreen's dream was accomplished.

Thus, the power of one.

An example of the power of one in my life occurred when a member of a women's ministry asked me to write a five- minute skit for an upcoming meeting. The skit was received well, and the plan was to continue the "series" for the next few meetings. Unfortunately, it was decided to discontinue the skits despite the success. Many of the women who attended were disappointed to learn that the project would end with the plot being undeveloped. I was faced with the question of should I allow it to fade away? It became clear that I needed to continue the series by turning it into a play. That five-minute skit has developed into two plays, three books, and approximately 100 video chats which are posted online.

Thus, the power of one.

Unfortunately, the power of one can also yield negative results. During my career as a Speech-Language Pathologist, I was invited to submit a proposal for a curriculum aimed to promote early literacy for preschool children. I agreed to design and modify the curriculum recognizing this would be a huge responsibility.

The project was phenomenally successful. The teachers, children, staff, and parents immediately became stakeholders. Although there was undeniable success proven by the data, it was decided that the curriculum would be discontinued.

In addition, several members of the leadership team attempted to sabotage the data by failing to hold teachers accountable for teaching the lessons correctly, as well as collecting, and reporting the data efficiently. Interestingly, I did travel to conferences and meet with other professionals on behalf of the agency. However, the one person with decision-making abilities regarding the curriculum allowed supervisors to discourage teachers from continuing the project with fidelity. The curriculum worked for the agency then and it continues to be effective many years later.

Keith Kent wrote in his book, *Anyway: The Paradoxical Commandments*,

"What you spend years building may be destroyed overnight, build anyway." page 27

A closing thought: When considering the power of one, do you empower or discourage? Let the good you do speak for you.

"Even so the tongue is a little member, and boasteth great things. Behold, how great a matter a little fire kindleth!

And the tongue is a fire, a world of iniquity: so is the tongue among our members, that it defileth the whole body, and setteth on fire the course of nature; and it is set on fire of hell.

James 3:5-6 (KJV)

BEWARE:
WORDS ARE IMPACTFUL

I often peruse my journal writings when feeling introspective. Recently, I came across an entry I penned years ago. My family was on a vacation with members of a church's congregation where we once attended. While waiting in the hotel's lobby to check-in at the front desk, a fellow congregant walked up to me and uttered the following, "You know, I've been entertaining evil thoughts about you." It blindsided me to the point that I became speechless. I remember laughing nervously, not giving a response. Later, the excuse for her behavior offered by others in the congregation alluded to the fact that she had mental illness. Whatever the case, it was a daunting experience. I am unaware of this woman's present condition, but I pray all is well with her.

Amazingly, on the same trip, another congregant became annoyed with the itinerary and lashed out to those who planned the excursion. Since my husband and I helped with planning the trip, we also became targets of her ire. She arose from her seat on the bus, looked at my husband and exclaimed," I don't like you, your wife, or your children." Well, so much for

I John 3:14 (KJV) which says,

"We know that we have passed from death unto life, because we love the brethren. He that loveth not his brother abideth in death."

In the book, *The Four Agreements Companion Book*, the author, Don Miguel Ruiz, implores the reader to *"Be impeccable with your word." page ix*

Be cognizant of the fact that the words spewing from your mouth cannot be retracted once entered in the atmosphere. Youth are particularly susceptible to words flung at them which can be injurious to their self-worth. This is one of the reasons why cyberbullying can be harmful to children and teenagers as they engage on social media.

Reflecting on the above discussion, are you impeccable with your words? Are you castigating, rude, condescending, aggressive, confrontational, or arrogant? Do you use words to bring peace or confusion to a situation? Some people are avoided because of their attitude and aren't pleasant to be around, but it is never expressed. In addition, there are those who may be experiencing a tough time and need a kind and encouraging word. It is always prudent to be intentional when addressing others. Remember,

"Beloved, let us love one another: for love is of God; and everyone that loveth is born of God, and knoweth God." I John 4:7 (KJV)

A closing thought: *"To laugh often and much: To win the respect of intelligent people and the affection of children, to earn the appreciation of honest critics and endure the betrayal of false friends; to appreciate beauty, to find the best in others, to leave the world a bit better whether by a healthy child, a garden patch, or a redeemed social condition; to know even one life has breathed easier because you lived. This is to have succeeded."*

Ralph Waldo Emerson

"The words of a talebearer are as wounds, and they go down into the innermost parts of the belly."

Proverbs 18:8 (KJV)

WHO ARE YOU LISTENING TO?

Have you heard the expression, "A dog who will bring a bone will carry a bone?" This was one of the many pearls of wisdom my mother shared with me. The message's intent is to be aware of those who tell you what someone else said about you. The question to be asked

Is, "What was your part in the conversation?" and "Why did they feel comfortable enough to talk with you about someone else?

Here are a few questions to consider:

- Do people seek you out for the purpose of castigating others?

- Do people seek you out for the purpose of abiding in chaos and confusion?

- Do people seek you out because gossiping is comfortable for you?

- Do people seek you out to assassinate the character of others?

Or

- Do people seek you out because you are an encourager?

- Do people seek you out because you are loving, compassionate, non-judgmental, empathetic, sympathetic, and a pleasure to be with?

- Do people seek you out because you have proven to be trustworthy with their innermost vulnerabilities and make confidentiality a priority?

Regrettably, many people have been betrayed because they shared intimate details of their life with those who did not have their best interests at heart. The resulting betrayal was devastating, and the "ride" was rough. I know because I've been there as well.

To conclude, who are you listening to and what are you telling others?

A closing thought: There are people who seek an audience to speak unflattering words against others. The question is, do they also speak unflattering words against you too? Avoid those conversations at all costs.

"I will praise thee; for I am fearfully and wonderfully made; marvellous are thy works; and that my soul knoweth right well."

Psalms 139:14 (KJV)

A PONDERING THOUGHT

The late Dr. Myles Munroe, pastor, teacher, and prolific writer frequently discussed a person's value in his books, sermons, and interviews. His message underscored the concept of value being determined by rarity. The rarer an object, it's value becomes exponentially greater. Understanding who you are and your value as a person mean that you become appreciative of who God created you to be, your very essence.

I have had conversations with people who confessed they have believed the opinions of others regarding their value and worth. A dangerous consequence of not knowing your value makes it easier to become a "people pleaser", relying on what others say or think about you while becoming self-deprecating. Ask yourself, "How is being a "people pleaser" working for you?" "Do you enjoy being a human doormat for someone else?" "Do you rather hide or withdraw so you don't face the possibility of being ostracized because you have the audacity to be authentically yourself?" Eleanor Roosevelt, wife of President Franklin Roosevelt of the United States and former First lady, was quoted saying, *"No one can make you feel inferior without your consent."*

Who are you at your core? Mary J. Blige, an American singer-songwriter and actress, released an album titled, *"Good Morning Gorgeous"*. Do you think to yourself, *"I love who I am"* upon seeing your reflection in the mirror? Do you walk through the world sharing your intrinsic values based upon whom God has created you to be? You are a precious gem, fashioned by God to be a gift to the world. The world is waiting for you to show up!

A closing thought: Value is not determined by conformity; it is determined by rarity.

"If it be possible, as much as lieth in you, live peaceably with all men."

Romans 12:18 (KJV)

RELATIONSHIPS

A friend confided in me that he had been experiencing a troubling situation related to his relationship with a good friend. He explained that he had been friends with this person for more than 40 years, and for an unknown reason, suddenly he wasn't returning his phone calls or answering his text messages. He said, "I've known him for a long time. I'm hurt and confused." Sadly, breaches occur in relationships for which there is no answer.

Recently, I saw a television commercial advertising an upcoming movie, titled "*Imaginary Friends.*" The title struck me because many people have had "imaginary friends". How many times have we had imaginary friends, relationships thought to be the pinnacle of relationship love? It is disturbing to discover that the bond you formed with a friend was one-sided, meaning that you may have been more of a true friend than the other. I have been blessed to have some true friendships lasting more than three decades. What a blessing! However, I've had friendships that were breached because of character assassination perpetrated upon me by others, for reasons unknown to me.

One of the most hurtful experiences I had regarding friendship was during my freshman year in college. I was told we would all meet for lunch and lighthearted conversation. To my amazement, one of my "imaginary friends" began the conversation by unleashing her perceptions of my personality to all those assembled. It became painfully clear that this was an attack, contrived to cause maximum damage to me and sabotage my relationship my other friends. Was it jealousy, envy, poor self-esteem, etc.? I didn't know then and I still don't know as of today why this happened? I do know it was memorable and never to be forgotten.

I'm also reminded of an incident I experienced regarding a relationship between me and a very good friend, a friend more like a sister. My brother passed away unexpectedly while he was out of town on a work assignment. After reaching my husband, I immediately thought of contacting family and friends. I especially thought of this friend since we had been confidants for each other, sharing intimate details of challenging life situations. I attempted to reach her by cell phone, work phone, and home phone to no avail. She didn't return my calls in a timely manner nor attend the funeral, visitation, or repast. I thought I would receive comfort and consolation from her but was met with silence. We never spoke about it but damage to the relationship had been done. The most difficult thing was to accept the breach without explanation.

Laurie Beth Jones, author of *Positive Prophecy*, recounted a story about a king and a snail she heard on National Public Radio. A snail tried unsuccessfully to reach the king's castle stairs several times but, was always kicked down. Finally, when the snail reached the king, he asked," *What was that all about?" page 233*

Frequently, all we're left with to mull over when faced with a relationship breach is "*What was that all about?*" Unfortunately, you may have to love the relationship partner from afar while letting go of what used to be. Circling back to the conversation with my friend, we concluded the discussion by appreciating the warm memories and the love shared with the partner which are indelibly marked in the heart.

So, how can you bridge separations caused by breaches in relationships? It can be swept under the proverbial rug or confronted to foster healing. One of my favorite television shows was *Queen Sugar* which aired on the OWN network. During the series, viewers were introduced to the characters, Aunt Vi, the matriarch of the Bordelon family, and her niece-in-law, Darla, who was now married to Ralph-Angel, Aunt Vi's nephew. An example of fostering healing was perfectly shown in season 7 and episode 3, titled "*Slowly and Always Irregularly*". Prior to Darla and Ralph-Angel marrying,

Aunt Vi ostracized Darla because of her challenges with addiction, among other things. Aunt Vi had been fiercely determined to protect Ralph-Angel from any potential hurts he may have suffered after he reconciled with Darla. During the episode, Aunt Vi spoke directly with Darla and said,

> "*I hate to think I might be one of the people that make you feel like you still had to earn your way into this community and I'm sorry for that, but now is the time to stand tall and know your worth.*"

I once offered an apology to someone during a tense moment in our relationship, although I did not know what I had done to cause the offense. The apology was not accepted, and the relationship remained damaged. I did all I could do by extending an olive branch to heal the breach. I gave myself grace myself and the other person grace anyway and hoped healing would come with the passing of time.

A closing thought: Sometimes people grow apart. However, if there is an offense, affirm the person's feelings, offer an apology, wish him or her well, and move on. Stay true to yourself. If there hasn't been something you may have done to cause the offense, give yourself and the other person grace and perhaps time will bring about healing.

Friendships are important, but so is discernment. Betrayal of trust may cause a hardened heart, one that is unwilling to form new relationships. I wrote in my book, *Thoughts to Ponder: Discovering your Authentic Self*,

> "*To trust is the willingness to be vulnerable and to be vulnerable is having the courage to trust. So many of us have trusted the wrong person and the betrayal was devastating.*" page 49

I continue to believe that genuine loving friendships are gifts to be protected. Never allow someone else's negative behavior to change your ability to remain your authentic self. I believe a hardened heart weakens the soul, your very essence.

"And be not conformed to this world: but be ye transformed by the renewing of your mind, that ye may prove what is that good, and acceptable, and perfect, will of God."

Romans 12:2 (KJV)

GIVE YOURSELF GRACE

I am human and because I am, I'm not perfect. My journey of self-discovery has been revelatory, enlightening, contemplative, and insightful. The process has revealed long ago memories of decisions made in my life that were not good ones, leaving a trail of repercussions in its wake. The reality is the past nor the negative outcomes can be changed. I think of those experiences as lessons in what not to do in the future.

Implicit in this discussion is seeking God for repentance and forgiveness, relying on the Holy Spirit to guide your daily walk. Remember *Psalms 37:23-24 (KJV),*

"The steps of a good man are ordered by the Lord: and he delighteth in his way.
Though he fall, he shall not be utterly cast down: for the Lord upholdeth him with his hand."

I have had to learn to give myself grace for not making better decisions at a given time. May I offer the following suggestions you are faced with the negative consequences because of unhealthy decisions:

- Repent and ask God for forgiveness
- Be mindful to not repeat poor decisions
- Forgive yourself for not knowing better at the time
- Forgive yourself for giving your power away to someone who was not worthy

- Forgive yourself for the unhealthy patterns you picked up while enduring or recovering from trauma

- Forgive others by extending grace to them when warranted

A closing thought: Once you learn better, do better. The decision is yours and yours alone.

PART THREE

Ebbs and Flows

"And we know that all things work together for good to them that love God, to them who are the called according to his purpose."

Romans 8:28 (KJV)

ARE YOU A SQUIRREL IN THE DESERT?

Everything Happens for a Reason is a book written by Mia Kirsch Kirschenbaum, whose parents and some family members were Holocaust survivors. The chapter titled, '*Squirrels in the desert: To help you feel at home in the world*", explored the idea that squirrels are comfortable in "a world of trees' rather than in a desert. She added,

> *"There are so many people who are miserable because they are squirrels in the desert." page 46*

God has created each one of us with a specific purpose. To live a quality life means discovering that purpose so God's will for our lives will be met. The late Dr. Myles Munroe wrote in his book, *Understanding your Potential*,

> *"The key to life is in the source of life itself, not in the life itself. Remember, the intentions of a creator is more important than that which is invented. Where use is not known, abuse is inevitable."* page 22

You are heavenly- designed and it is your uniqueness that is a blessing to the others. You have been fashioned and shaped to possess what's needed for your life's work. Therefore, never accept the beliefs of those who are antagonistic to your goals, missions, dreams, and visions. Everyone is not going to accept your purpose or missions. There are those whose intentions are to sabotage your assignments by whatever means at their disposal. Nevertheless, solidify your purpose and perform your missions to the glory of God.

Let's just endeavor to be ourselves. Why become the embodiment of another when you are perfect just as we are?

A closing thought: "Purpose is wrapped up in who you are. No one else can do what God put you here to do. You are unique. You are special. You are an original.

Chase your purpose by just embracing who you are.

You have everything you need to pursue your purpose.

Believe that! Walk in that! "

Ahna Alisia Patterson

"To everything there is a season, and a time to every purpose under the heaven:

A time to be born, and a time to die; a time to plant, and a time to pluck up that which is planted;

A time to kill, and a time to heal; a time to break down, and a time to build up;

A time to weep, and a time to laugh; a time to mourn, and a time to dance;

A time to cast away stones, and a time to gather stones together; a time to embrace, and a time to refrain from embracing;

A time to get, and a time to lose; a time to keep, and a time to cast away;

A time to rend, and a time to sew; a time to keep silence, and a time to speak;

A time to love, and a time to hate; a time of war, and a time of peace,"

Ecclesiastes 3:1-8 (KJV)

WINTER, SPRING, SUMMER, OR FALL

It is my sincerest endeavor to show up and present myself to the world as whom God has created me to be. Pure and simple. However, there have been times when difficult situations caused a temporary shift in my attitude or mood. Nevertheless, it is my desire to bring love and peace wherever I go. I make every effort to be kind, compassionate, empathetic, sympathetic, encouraging, and pleasant to be around.

This thought reminded me of seasonal changes and the characteristics of each. During the winter, the temperature is usually cold which slows plant growth. Spring is known for the adage, "April's showers bring May flowers". Summer tends to have the warmest temperatures and most daylight, yielding an abundance of flowers and plants. Hence, seasons represent change, crucial for nature to thrive.

Reflecting on the above discussion, I began to use the seasons as a metaphor for how one may show up in the world. Frequently, external forces such as the death of a loved one, financial difficulties, health concerns, job losses, betrayals which result in relationship breaches, altering one's personality or mood. Considering the seasons, perhaps one may show up as:

- Winter- Always gloomy, never positive, incapable of finding the good in others, with a dark cloud surrounding your essence?

- Spring – Sometimes cloudy, with intermittent showers of "gloom" or sunny with the prospect of seeing a rainbow indicating a glimmer of hopefulness?

- Summer – Sunny, with a shine so bright that a tense environment will become calmer; like a breath of fresh air with a mild breeze blowing; minimal humidity of tears; recognizing that a hurricane or tropical storm may form and wreak havoc but knowing it is temporary and conditions will temper soon?

- Fall – Like a chameleon, changing like the leaves on a tree; trying to "fit in" so as not to be isolated from others; becoming an imitation for a moment in time, rather than remaining authentic and genuine?

One of my favorite television shows is "*Dr. Foster*", a British series aired on BritBox. During one rather intensely emotional scene, Dr. Foster and her friend were having a contentious discussion regarding infidelity in season 1 and episode 5 titled, "A woman scorned." It was revealed that Dr. Foster had slept with her friend's husband. The friend, peering at Dr. Foster with a very cold blank stare while holding a glass of wine said,

"You have no idea how you come across; what people say when you leave the room. They breathe a sigh of relief because I don't know if you mean to, but you make them feel uncomfortable. And even though you say you like them, it's clear you think you're slightly better than all of us."

I concede the notion that Dr. Foster had previously made poor decisions, including having an adulterous affair with her friend. Perhaps the friend may have been harsh with Dr. Foster because of the betrayal she felt, or as a projection of her own feelings, but the message was clear that Dr. Foster was not a pleasant or nice person.

I yearn to show up like summer, aware that I may sometimes resemble the characteristics of winter, spring, or fall. To be certain that my presence brings love, peace, calm, and grace to situations, although they may not be reciprocated. It's my heart's desire to leave a place better than when I found it, because I was there.

A closing thought: All seasons are necessary but each one opens the path for renewal and rejuvenation.

"Be careful for nothing; but in every thing by prayer and supplication with thanksgiving let your requests be made known unto God.

"And the peace of God, which passeth all understanding, shall keep your hearts and minds through Christ Jesus."

Philippians 4:6-7 (KJV)

NO HEAVY LIFTING

My graduate school experience was an intriguing one. The Anatomy and Physiology class included dissections which weren't all that unusual. What was unusual was that the dissections were not frogs, pigs, or sheep hearts. We dissected cadavers. One of my classmates would say, "Real-life dead people!". As our lab group worked our way through the body, the skin layers, (epidermis, dermis, and hypodermis),and fascia had to be cut open to reveal the skeletal and muscular systems, as well as the internal organs.

During the birth of two of my children, it became necessary that the delivery would have to be through Caesarean sections (C-sections). Post-delivery, my doctor advised that there should be no heavy lifting or driving. Why? Because if there was a physical assault to my body, the healing process may have been endangered. Healing takes place from the inside out and not from the skin to the inside of the body. Having experienced dissections, I could clearly understand the importance of this advice. Medication was prescribed for pain and rest was also critical.

So how can we connect these two things - physical and emotional pain? A person may have endured physical pain if a bandage or limping is present. However, a person's emotional pain may not be manifested. It may be suppressed and minimized, not easily detectable. It can be overshadowed by using self-destructive ways to self-medicate the pain.

To reiterate, what is a crucial component of the healing process after a surgery or injury? No heavy lifting. By avoiding this activity, one can prevent the wound from opening and thereby escaping possible infection. What is a crucial component of the healing process after suffering emotional pain? Avoid heavy lifting. Heavy lifting comes in the form of triggering events. And why should you avoid triggering events after suffering emotional trauma? Triggering events open emotional wounds which lead to depression, anxiety, isolation, and dependence on addictive behaviors.

It is imperative to seek God and spiritual support when faced with emotional pain. In addition, medical treatment and professional counseling are often necessary to promote healing. Avoid negative and toxic situations and people, rethink and eliminate vengeance from your mental rolodex, and reject emotionally challenging scripts in your mind by using the delete button. Be kind to yourself, forgive yourself for the "slip-ups" in your life, and learn to love others.

A closing thought: No one is excluded from physical or emotional pain. However, emotional pain exposes vulnerability and expresses the need to recognize that there's an innermost deeper problem which must be addressed. Unresolved pain is damaging to mind and heart, ultimately preventing the life God has for you. God is waiting to soothe and medicate your broken places so open your heart to Him. He's not too busy to bless you!

> *"Finally, brethren, whatsoever things are true, whatsoever things are honest, whatsoever things are just, whatsoever things are pure, whatsoever things are lovely, whatsoever things are of good report; if there be any virtue, and if there be any praise, think on these things."*
> *Phillipians 4:8 (KJV)*

"For I am persuaded, that neither death, nor life, nor angels, nor principalities, nor powers, nor things present, nor things to come,
Nor height, nor depth, nor any other creature, shall be able to separate us from the love of God, which is in Christ Jesus our Lord."

Romans 8:38-39 (KJV)

SHATTERED GLASS

A couple of years ago, I read *The Boy, the Mole, the Fox, and the Horse* written by Charlie Mackesy, a book of entirely handwritten quips, quotes, and wise thoughts. One such question asked by the mole when he saw the boy was, *"Is your glass half empty or half full?"* The boy's response was, *"I think I'm grateful to have a glass."*

Initially, I was struck by the boy's answer implying that he had a posture of gratitude. However, as I meditated on the discussion, I wondered, "What happens when the glass one has breaks? Will the person have the intestinal fortitude or the temerity to get another glass?" So many times, we've been shattered into a million pieces, just like glass. The question remains, how do we begin to put the shards of glass back together?

CBS Sunday Morning featured a dog named Dexter, who was hit by a car, causing the loss of one of his front legs with the other to be paralyzed. He was outfitted with a "doggie walker with wheels", but Dexter didn't like it. So, what did he do? He rebranded himself by ridding himself of the obstacle in his way. Dexter began walking on his hind legs, so he was now in an upright position. He was now a celebrity in his town!

Vehicle navigational systems are commonplace today. They are relied upon to find the best route for a given destination. Sometimes, the driver is advised to follow a detour because of road construction, accidents, or other obstacles in the way. However, if the detour is followed, it will ultimately lead back to the original road.

There may have been obstacles that have changed the trajectory of your life. Knowing how to handle the "detours" will help you to overcome the adversities. It may not be easy due to bumpy roads, unfamiliar territory, or unexpected delays in reaching in your destination. Think about Dexter, who let go of his front legs and decided to meet the adversity by using what he had left, his hind legs.

One of the most difficult periods in my life was during my late mother's health journey. It began with her having brain surgery, resulting in years of debilitation, ultimately requiring a cerebral shunt to relieve excess fluid in her brain. One day, as I was tending to her at her bedside, she grabbed my hand, pulled me in closer, looked at me intensely, and said, "You can only do what you can do." I knew, at that moment, that her mother's intuition recognized my stress level had hit a fever pitch and I was drowning.

During this time, my husband had a corporate job which demanded long work hours, my children were 7, 9 and 14 years of age, and I was building my professional career. In addition to these factors, because of relationship breaches in my extended family, the lack of expected family support further impacted my anxiety level. Oftentimes, there are periods in our lives when we are faced with situations which are far beyond our control. This was such a time since I did not have control over my mother's debilitating health. I truly was not prepared for the road I was traveling.

Another challenging event happened when I experienced a very painful loss as I was writing this book. It was so unexpected that I became overcome with grief. The event was dizzying resulting in a shift to the balance of my emotions. Metaphorically speaking, I liken it to the diagnosis of vertigo, a condition affecting the inner ear. It was incredibly frightening because everything was spinning around me. Significant emotional events can without a doubt, affect your balance.

The ebbs and flows of life can create a tsunami of emotions causing us to become a casualty of this perilous journey called life. Some events that occur in our lives may be catastrophic enough to last a lifetime, others, for a moment in time. I implore you to remain attached to God, praying for His grace and mercy as you traverse the emotional jungle in your mind. The process of conquering adversities may take days, months, or years. But continue the process by seeking God for the wisdom needed to overcome. Remember, all advice is not the best advice. *Psalms 1:1* (KJV) clearly says,

"Blessed is the man that walketh not in the counsel of the ungodly, nor standeth in the way of sinners, nor sitteth in the seat of the scornful."

I have never forgotten my mother's advice and the look in her eyes. Frequently, I reflect on the Serenity Prayer written by Dr. Reinhold Niebuhr:

"O God and Heavenly Father, grant to us the serenity of mind to accept that which cannot be changed, courage to change that which can be changed, and wisdom to know the one from the other through Jesus Christ, our Lord."
Amen

Always remember that our hope and peace are in God. Control what you can and leave the rest to Jesus.

"Come unto me, all ye that labour and are heavy laden, and I will give you rest.
Take my yoke upon you, and learn of me; for I am meek and lowly in heart: and ye shall find rest unto your souls.
For my yoke is easy, and my burden is light."
Matthew 11: 28-30 (KJV)

A closing thought: Life is a journey, replete with obstacles, challenges, and lessons along the way. The question is whether belief in ourselves and self-awareness will help to weather the storms or is giving up constantly on a feedback loop in our minds?

Detours are temporary. Your purpose is set, God-ordained. Follow the path set for you knowing that your steps are ordered.

Be blessed!

"Now the God of hope fill you with all joy and peace in believing, that ye may abound in hope, through the power of the Holy Ghost."

Romans 15:13 (KJV)

HOPELESS AND HOMELESS

Communities today are being confronted with the dilemma of solving the challenge of homelessness, whether it is the result of poverty, mental illness, or drug addiction. Regardless of the cause, local and federal governmental agencies grappling with the issue, find the solution to the problem to be a daunting task.

Many of the unhoused population, tend to resort to panhandling for survival. They display signs with messages like, "I'll work for food", Veteran need help", or sometimes boldly declaring, "I need a beer." During a vacation to Chicago, while walking on Miracle Mile, my family was approached by a man panhandling whose constant refrain was, *"Can you spare me 30 cents?"* His tactic was novel indeed.

Recently, a man who usually stakes out a very busy intersection near my home, displayed a sign with a message that read, "Hopeless and homeless." I was disturbed by the sign because it's implicit meaning was that he had lost faith, believing that all hope was gone. Seemingly, his appreciation for life had diminished to the point that he assumed his current situation had not and would not change. One of the most unfortunate realities of people experiencing calamities, adversities, or hardships, is that there is little belief in the possibility that a life-altering event improve their status.

An excerpt from an essay titled "Faith", in my book, *Thoughts to Ponder: Discovering your Authentic Self*, reads:

"*It (hope) is living in a perpetual state of expectation. There may be a period in our lives that seem hopeless, which requires renewal, leading to rejuvenation. To hope is to remain steadfast, resilient, and resistant to the urge to give up during difficult times. Sometimes, hope represents a time of great anticipation, resulting in extended moments of delight and joy.*
It is our faith that determines our hope, perseverance, confidence, and tenacity to know that everything will be alright." page 42

Let us not become numb to those who may be displaying signs with messages of hopelessness. They are not invisible; they are a part of humanity. Their lives may have been interrupted by unforeseen circumstances or poor decisions, but it doesn't mean they are of no significance or purpose.

Everyone is created by God, in His image and likeness, and it is therefore irrefutable, that all are valuable!

A closing thought: "*But by the grace of God I am what I am: and his grace which was bestowed upon me was not in vain; but I laboured more abundantly than they all: yet not I, but the grace of God which was with me.*" *I Corinthians 15:10 (KJV)*

"And be not conformed to this world: but be ye transformed by the renewing of your mind, that ye may prove what is that good, and acceptable, andperfect, will of God."

Romans12:2-3 (KJV)

PRISON WALLS

Several years ago, a friend of mine lamented that it took prison walls to turn his life around. He expressed a determination to not allow this misstep in life to predict his present or future life. As our conversations became more intense, his deep-seated emotions seeped in, layer upon layer. It became clear that his intention was to avoid situations and decisions which led to his incarceration. He became a student of God's word and an ardent follower of Jesus Christ.

During one of our conversations, my friend told me some of the inmates preferred to remain incarcerated because it was a familiar environment. Freedom was not always welcomed, and prison walls became their "natural habitat." Prison walls are certainly restrictive, but what are the manifestations of mental prison walls? Included are intimidation, self-doubt, unresolved painful memories, abuse, negative self-esteem, rejection, fear of failure, and/or abandonment. The thought that shame and embarrassment is in the background waiting to pounce if missions, goals, dreams, or vision are not realized.

Frequently, I include a metamorphosis theme with my students. At the conclusion of the project, once the butterflies hatch, it is exciting to prepare to release them from their habitat. On the day of release, all five of the butterflies were expected to fly out of the habitat immediately; however, only four flew without hesitation. One remained although the students shook the habitat vigorously, attempting to coax it fly with the others. But the last butterfly continued feasting on the fruit that was left. Finally, after several minutes, it flew out of the habitat with little prompting. As I recounted the story to my family, my sound remarked, "That is what bondage looks like when freedom is available."

Stepping outside of a comfort zone can be intimidating since it represents an unknown place ladled with unknown expectations. Prison walls are certainly physical, but they can also be a mental representation of a troubled mind, a mind in bondage. The mind can play an ominous game eventually perpetuating a self-defeatist attitude, with the person unable to visualize the endless possibilities life can afford. Wouldn't you rather free yourself from the bondage of mental prison walls and fly free?

A closing thought: Explore your God-given purpose, gifts, and talents. It may require leaving your physical or mental comfort zone, but the cell door of bondage will be unlocked, and you will fly just as that last butterfly did when you realize that freedom is available, if you dare to seek it.

"If any of you lack wisdom, let him ask of God, that giveth to all men liberally, and upbraideth not; and it shall be given him."

James 1:5 (KJV))

DECISIONS

For several years, I hosted a summer camp for youth in grades PreK – middle school. On the first day of camp, I made the decision to discuss consequences by taking a page from B.F. Skinner's operant conditioning theory about stimulus, response, and consequence. I told each class to write their classroom rules related to behavior. I said, "If a situation is presented to you and you become angry, defying authority, I want you to think about how you're going to respond because your response is going to dictate your consequence, be it positive or negative."

I further explained that there may be incidents when someone pushes or hits another camper, uses inappropriate language, is disrespectful to staff, destroys camp property, takes another camper's property, etc. That's the stimulus. The question is, what is going to be the response? They decided some of the consequences would be to lose field trip privileges, several minutes of recreation or swim time, meaning everyone would be in the pool, but the camper would have to sit out with camp counselors. The loss of swim time was by far the most devastating consequence.

Dr. Steven Covey, in his book, *The 7 Habits of Highly Effective People*, explained how Victor Frankl, a psychiatrist, Jew, and a prisoner in Nazi Germany, was instrumental in his thought process related to stimulus, response, and the gap between them. Dr. Covey wrote,

"I read the paragraph over and over again. It basically contained the simple idea that there is a gap or space between stimulus and response, and that the key to both our growth and happiness is how we use that space." page 310

One day, a camper became frustrated with a peer and engaged in a pushing -match. I asked the camper to tell me the rules about physical altercations. He said he wouldn't be allowed to attend the upcoming field trip. I agreed and he returned to his class. Later that day, another one of his peers came to me and asked, "Miss Kathy, how can he redeem himself?" I was taken by her empathy; however, I explained that I wouldn't override the class rules. The decision to reverse the consequence would have to be made by the class. The class discussed the situation and the camper apologized. His peers voted to rescind the consequence so the camper would be allowed to attend the field trip. Unfortunately, the camper's parent refused to allow him to attend the field trip because of the altercation.

There are life's decisions that must be made. It is imperative to stop for a moment when a stimulus is given, reflect on the response during the gap, and then make the decision.

A decision made have far reaching consequences, positive or negative, and change the course of one's life. Consequences can bring joy or peace, chaos, or confusion.

So, the next time you're faced with a challenging situation, remember one unwise response can alter the trajectory of your life.

A closing thought: Hear; listen; think; reflect. Now act!

INTERACTIVE JOURNAL

PURPOSE MAY BE CORRUPTED
BUT NEVER DESTROYED: PART I

Would you give again to someone who has taken advantage of your compassion and kindness?

_____

_____

_____

_____

_____

_____

If no, why not?

_____

_____

_____

_____

_____

If yes, what boundaries and limitations would you put in place?

_____

_____

_____

_____

_____

PURPOSE MAY BE CORRUPTED
BUT NEVER DESTROYED: PART II

What obstacles have you allowed to distract you from pursuing your missions, goals, or vision?

_____

_____

_____

_____

_____

_____

_____

Who are the "encouragers" in your life? How do they support you?

_____

_____

_____

_____

_____

_____

_____

Have you ever been told you're not capable of achieving a mission, goal, or vision? When?

_____

_____

_____

_____

_____

_____

_____

If yes, what did it take for you to ignore the negativity and forge ahead anyway?

_____

_____

_____

_____

_____

_____

_____

_____

BE WHO YOU ARE, NO MATTER THE SITUATION

What negative self-talk have you had to silence?

_____

_____

_____

_____

_____

_____

_____

What painful experiences have you faced which contributed to SWID? How are you handling them?

_____

_____

_____

_____

_____

_____

_____

I KNOW WHO I AM

When have you camouflaged yourself to fit in with people?

_____

_____

_____

_____

_____

_____

_____

_____

How has God sustained you during difficult periods in your life?

_____

_____

_____

_____

_____

_____

_____

_____

REFLECT AND MEDITATE

Now is a good time to remind yourself of your life's purpose. Write it here.

_____

_____

_____

_____

_____

_____

_____

What missions are you contemplating?

_____

_____

_____

_____

_____

_____

Are you willing to fulfill the mission despite setbacks?

_____

_____

_____

_____

_____

_____

_____

BETRAYAL OF LOVE: STAY TRUE TO YOURSELF

Do you think the opposite of love is hate or suffering? Why?

_____

_____

_____

_____

_____

_____

_____

Have you ever experienced unrequited love?

_____

_____

_____

_____

_____

_____

_____

THE STRENGTH OF COURAGE IS DETERMINED BY THE OF ONE'S CONVICTIONS

Have you ever had to be courageous when your convictions were attacked? How did you handle the situation?

_____

_____

_____

_____

_____

_____

_____

_____

When do you think debating a controversial topic is necessary?

_____

_____

_____

_____

_____

_____

_____

_____

PURPOSE, MISSION, AND INTENTIONS

Reminder: Rewrite your purpose here.

_____

_____

_____

_____

_____

_____

_____

_____

Have you discontinued pursuing a mission that no longer aligns with your purpose? If yes, why?

_____

_____

_____

_____

_____

_____

_____

_____

BE MINDFUL OF YOUR DAILY WALK

Have you ever been "church hurt" by a fellow member of a congregation to which you belonged?

_____

_____

_____

_____

_____

_____

Was the situation rectified? If yes, how?

_____

_____

_____

_____

_____

_____

If no, why not?

_____

_____

_____

_____

_____

_____

THE POWER OF ONE

When was the "power of one" a positive experience in your life?

_____

_____

_____

_____

_____

_____

_____

When was the "power of one" a negative experience in your life?

_____

_____

_____

_____

_____

_____

_____

_____

BEWARE: WORDS ARE IMPACTFUL

Have you ever apologized for berating someone during a private conversation or in the presence of others? Was the apology accepted?

_____

_____

_____

_____

_____

_____

_____

_____

Has anyone ever apologized to you for using offensive language toward you in a private conversation or in the presence of others? Did you accept the apology?

_____

_____

_____

_____

_____

_____

_____

_____

WHO ARE YOU LISTENING TO?

What types of conversations do you enjoy mostly?

_____
_____
_____
_____
_____
_____
_____
_____

What types of conversations do you avoid?

_____
_____
_____
_____
_____
_____
_____
_____

PONDERING THOUGHTS

Have you ever been a "people pleaser?" Have you moved on from that sentiment or are you still stuck there?

_____

_____

_____

_____

_____

_____

_____

How do you avoid camouflaging yourself to "fit in" with others?

_____

_____

_____

_____

_____

_____

_____

When was the last time you felt it necessary to camouflage yourself in a group of people?

_____

_____

_____

_____

_____

_____

_____

RELATIONSHIPS

Have you ever attempted to repair a relationship breach and it was not accepted?

_____

_____

_____

_____

_____

_____

_____

_____

Has anyone ever caused a relationship breach with you which was so egregious, you found it difficult to repair?

_____

_____

_____

_____

_____

_____

_____

_____

GIVE YOURSELF GRACE

When did you have to give yourself grace for dealing with the consequences of a poor decision?

_____

_____

_____

_____

_____

_____

_____

_____

When did someone give you grace for a poor decision you made which had a negative impact?

_____

_____

_____

_____

_____

_____

_____

_____

ARE YOU A SQUIRREL IN A DESERT?

What environment do you feel the most comfortable?

_____

_____

_____

_____

_____

_____

_____

What environment do you feel the least comfortable?

_____

_____

_____

_____

_____

_____

_____

HOW DO YOU SHOW UP? WINTER, SPRING, SUMMER, OR FALL?

What season do you represent most?

_____

_____

_____

_____

_____

_____

_____

What season do you represent the least?

_____

_____

_____

_____

_____

_____

Are you a combination of the seasons?

_____

_____

_____

_____

_____

_____

_____

NO HEAVY LIFTING

What emotional pain has left you bereft of joy and/or happiness?

_____

_____

_____

_____

_____

_____

_____

_____

What have you done to ease or soothe the pain?

_____

_____

_____

_____

_____

_____

_____

Have these strategies worked?

_____

_____

_____

_____

_____

_____

If not, what can you do to heal?

_____

_____

_____

_____

_____

_____

_____

_____

SHATTERED GLASS

When was your faith shaken?

_____

_____

_____

_____

_____

_____

_____

_____

How did you recover?

_____

_____

_____

_____

_____

_____

_____

HOPELESS AND HOMELESS

Do you live in a state of expectation and hope or pessimism?

_____

_____

_____

_____

_____

_____

_____

What do you do to increase your optimism?

_____

_____

_____

_____

_____

_____

_____

PRISON WALLS

How do you battle the prison walls in your mind to fight against insecurity, the feelings of "not enough", poor self-image, negative self-talk, or low self-esteem?

_____

_____

_____

_____

_____

_____

_____

When was the last time you declared, "Enough is enough!" when faced with feelings of "not being enough"?

_____

_____

_____

_____

_____

_____

_____

NOTES

PART ONE

Patterson, K. (2022). *Thoughts to Ponder: Discovering your Authentic Self* (Pennsauken, New Jersey: Book Baby) 34

Patterson, K.(2022) *Thoughts to Ponder: Discovering your Authentic Self* (Pennsauken, New Jersey: Book Baby) 43

Gladwell, M. (2008) *Outliers* (New York, New York: Little, brown, and Company, a division of Hachette Book Group, Inc.) 19

Brown, B. (2020, October 24). *"Ultimate betrayal". YouTube.* Retrieved 6/20/2024 from https://www.youtube.com results?search_query=brene+brown+ultimate+betrayal

"Popeye the Sailor". (Last revision 2024, June 20) Wikipedia, the free encyclopedia
Retrieved 6/20/2024 from https://en.wikipedia.org/wiki/Popeye

PART TWO

Pinkney, J. (2000) *Aesop Fables* (San Francisco, California: Chronicle Books, LLC) 36

Kennedy, J. (1956) *Profiles in Courage* (New York, New York: Harper and Brothers) xvii

Ginott, H. (1972) *Teacher and Child* (United Kingdom, MacMillan Company) 15

"Why did Gandhi say, "If it weren't for Christians, I'd be a Christian" *(2016, August 10). Kansas City Star.* Retrieved 6/60/2024 from https://www.vvdailypress.com/story/lifestyle/faith/2016/08/26/ why-did-gandhi-say-x2018/985856007

Patterson, K. (2022). *Thoughts to Ponder: Discovering your Authentic Self* (Pennsauken, New Jersey: Book Baby) 49

Patterson, K. (1997) *I am a* Jewel (Harvey, Louisiana: Self-Published) 22

"Jazz Clarinetist Doreen Ketchens plays her dream gig". (2023, May 28). *YouTube.* CBS Sunday Morning. Retrieved 6/20/2024 from https://www.youtube.com/ results?search_query=doreen+ketchens+cbs+sunday+morning

Keith, K. (2004) *Anyway: The Paradoxical commandments* (New York, New York: Berkley Publishing Group, A division of Penguin Group USA0,Inc.) 27

Ruiz, D. (2000) *The four Agreements Companion Book* (San Rafael, California: Amber-Allen Publishing, Inc.) ix

Jones, L. (1999) *Positive Prophecy* (New York, New York: Hyperion) 233

PART THREE

Kirschbaum, M. (2004) *Everything Happens for a Reason* (New York, New York, MJF Books) 46

Munroe, M. (1991) *Understanding your Potential* (Shippensburg, Pennsylvania: Destiny Image Publishers) 22

Ava Duvernay (Writer), DeMane Davis (Director) (2022). *"Slowly and Always Irregularly".* In Queen Sugar Series (Season 7, Episode 3), Oprah Winfrey Network. Retrieved 6/20/2024 from Oprah.com/sp/queen-sugar.html

Mike Bartlett, (Writer), Jeremy Lovering (Director). (2015). *A woman scorned".* In Dr. Foster Series (Season 1, Episode 5), BritBox Retrieved 6/20/2024 from https://www.britbox.com/us/show/Doctor_Foster_b094m5t9

Mackesy, C. (2019) *The Boy, the Mole, the Fox, and the Horse* (New York, New York: First Harper One)

"One upstanding dog". CBS Sunday Morning, (2022, July 10) Retrieved 6/23/2024 from https://www.youtube.com/watch?v=vkNnd-JkM5Q

Patterson, K. (2022) *Thoughts to Ponder: Discovering your Authentic Self* (Pennsauken, New Jersey: Book Baby) 42

Covey, S. (1990) *The 7 Habits of Highly Effective People* (New York, New York: Simon and Schuster) 310